KU-268-848

The Two Ronnies

10 9 8 7 6 5 4 3 2 1

This edition published 2013

First published in 2003 by Ebury Press, an imprint of Ebury Publishing
A Random House Group company

Collection copyright © Ebury Press 2003

Copyright © Ronnie Barker, Peter Vincent, Ian Davidson, Spike Mullins 2003

Ronnie Barker, Peter Vincent, Ian Davidson and Spike Mullins have asserted
their right to be identified as the authors of this Work in accordance with the
Copyright, Designs and Patents Act 1988

All rights reserved. No part of this publication may be reproduced, stored in a
retrieval system, or transmitted in any form or by any means, electronic,
mechanical, photocopying, recording or otherwise, without the prior permission
of the copyright owner

The Random House Group Limited Reg. No. 954009

Addresses for companies within the Random House Group can be found at:
www.randomhouse.co.uk

A CIP catalogue record for this book is available from the British Library

The Random House Group Limited supports the Forest Stewardship Council® (FSC®),
the leading international forest-certification organisation. Our books carrying the
FSC label are printed on FSC®-certified paper. FSC is the only forest-certification
scheme supported by the leading environmental organisations, including Greenpeace.
Our paper procurement policy can be found at: www.randomhouse.co.uk/environment

Created by Essential Works
29 Clerkenwell Green, London, EC1R 0DU

Photographs: In The Chair and Tramps © BBC, all other images Ronnie Barker

Printed and bound by CPI Group (UK) Ltd, Croydon, CR0 4YY

ISBN 9780091958015

To buy books by your favourite authors and register for offers visit:
www.randomhouse.co.uk

The Two Ronnies

their funniest jokes, one-liners and sketches

Contents

COMEDY CLASSICS

Good Evening and in a Packed Show Tonight . . .

RB We'll be talking to a pathetic out-of-work contortionist who claims that he can't make ends meet.

RC And to a masochist who likes nothing better than a cold bath every morning – so he has a warm bath every evening.

RB And then a lady who's a world authority on carpets, an expert on rugs and not at all bad on lino.

RC Then we'll talk to a stereo expert about his favourite breakfast – two bowls of Rice Krispies ten feet apart.

RB　And a Sultan with 365 wives will explain why he's looking forward to leap year.

RC　Then we'll interview the Romford girl who took the Pill washed down with pond water and was today diagnosed as being three months stagnant.

RB　After that we'll be meeting a tax inspector who'll show us how to fill in a form, followed by a foreman who'll show us how to fill in a tax inspector.

RC　And a famous millionaire will reveal how it feels to have piles of gold – wealthy but uncomfortable.

RB   Then we'll feature the famous colour-blind poet, Mr Reginald Smithers. Here's an excerpt from one of his poems:

RC   *Roses are red*
Violets are brown
The sky is bright yellow
And so are bluetits

RB   And now a sketch featuring Mr Ronnie Corbett, who this year made a lot of money on the greyhounds – as a jockey.

In the Divorce Court Today

RC A husband claimed that his wife's mother kept shouting at him that he was driving too fast along the M1 – and to make matters worse she swore at him while he was untying her from the roof rack.

RB And an executive from a toothpaste manufacturing company was divorced by his wife on the grounds of cruelty. She claimed he kept squeezing her at the wrong end.

RC Then Madame Fifi Dubonnet, the former Picasso model, claimed that last Sunday her husband severely assaulted her and gave her three black eyes.

Later We'll Discuss the Burning Questions . . .

RC . . . What should you tip the porter in an all-male nudist camp – and will a fiver cover it?

RB Pilfering coal miners – do they have lots of slack in their trousers?

RC Education – can cross-eyed teachers control their pupils?

RB   Then we'll be discussing potholing and why it ruins your bedroom carpets.

RC   And a very wealthy man who was a snow-plough driver in Trinidad will tell us how he fiddled his overtime.

RB   Then we'll consider loneliness, with a special report from the Archbishop of Golders Green.

RC And for ladies we'll be talking about rum babas – and what to wear if you've got them.

RB We'll be discussing our new Classic series – *What Katy Did, What Katy Did Next, Who Did What to Katy* and *Son of Katy*.

RC Which will lead us to discuss three famous oriental sex books, the Kama Sutra, The Less Calm Sutra and The Absolutely Frantic Sutra.

COMEDY CLASSICS

Fork Handles
or 'Annie Finkhouse?'

An old ironmonger's shop. A shop that sells everything – garden equipment, ladies' tights, builders' supplies, mousetraps – everything. A long counter up and down stage. A door to the back of the shop up left. The back wall also has a counter. Lots of deep drawers and cupboards up high, so that RC has to get a ladder to get some of the goods RB orders. RC is serving a woman with a toilet roll. He is not too bright.

RC   There you are – mind how you go.

Woman exits. RB enters – a workman. Not too bright either.

RC   Yes, sir?

RB Four candles?

RC Four candles? Yes, sir. *(He gets four candles from a drawer.)* There you are.

RB No – fork handles.

RC Four candles. That's four candles.

RB No, fork handles – handles for forks.

RC Oh, fork handles. *(He gets a garden fork handle from the back of the shop.)* Anything else?

RB *(Looks at his list.)* Got any plugs?

RC What sort of plugs?

RB Bathroom – rubber one.

RC gets box of bath plugs, holds up two different sizes.

RC What size?

RB Thirteen amp.

RC Oh, electric plugs. *(Gets electric plug from drawer.)* What else?

RB Saw tips.

RC Sore tips? What you want, ointment?

RB No, tips to cover the saw.

RC Oh. No, we ain't got any.

RB Oh. Got any hose?

RC Hoes? Yeah. *(He gets a garden hoe from the garden department.)*

RB No – hose.

RC Oh, hose. I thought you meant hoes. *(He gets a roll of garden hose.)*

RB No – hose.

RC   *(Gives him a dirty look.)* What hose? *(He gets a packet of ladies' tights from a display stand.)* Pantyhose, you mean?

RB   No, 'O's – letter 'O's – letters for the gate. 'Mon Repose'.

RC   Why didn't you say so? *(He gets ladder, climbs up to cupboard high up on wall, gets down box of letters.)* Now, 'O's – here we are – two?

RB   Yeah.

RC   Right. *(He takes box back up ladder and returns.)* Next?

RB   Got any 'P's?

RC Oh, my Gawd. Why didn't you bleedin' say while I'd got the box of letters down here? I'm working me guts out here climbing about all over the shop, putting things back and then getting 'em out again. Now then, *(he is back with the box)* how many? Two?

RB No – peas – three tins of peas.

RC You're having me on, ain't yer? Ain't yer! *(He gets three tins of peas.)*

RB No, I ain't. I meant tinned peas.

RC Right. Now what?

RB Pumps.

RC Pumps? Hand pumps or foot pumps?

RB Foot.

RC Footpumps. Right. *(He goes off, returns with a small footpump.)* Right.

RB No, pumps for your feet. Brown pumps, size nine.

RC You are having me on. I've had enough of this. *(He gets them from drawer.)* Is that the lot?

RB Washers?

RC *(exasperated)* Windscreen washers? Car washers? Dishwashers? Hair washers? Back scrubbers? Lavatory cleaners? Floor washers?

RB Half-inch washers.

RC Tap washers! Here, give me that list, I'm fed up with this. *(He reads list and reacts)* Right! That does it. That's the final insult. *(Calls through door)* Elsie! Come and serve this customer – I've had enough!

RC stalks off. Elsie enters – a big, slovenly woman with a very large bosom. She takes the list. Reads it.

ELSIE Right, sir – what sort of knockers are you looking for?

Sports News

RB In the transatlantic single-handed yacht race Mr Owen Smithers has been disqualified for using both hands.

RC Tonight's tug of war between England and France may have to be cancelled if nobody can find a twenty-six-mile rope.

In Social News

RC Short-sighted Lady Myopia Fotheringay was in the news again when she opened the new haberdashery centre at Slough by cutting a ceremonial ribbon. As she did so, a large crowd cheered and her knickers fell down.

RB The wedding took place in Pinewood today of Sylvia Lummox, for twenty-seven years a cinema usherette. The organist played selections from *The Sound of Music*; during the sermon the sidesman sold ice cream and the bride herself, all in white, came down the aisle backwards, waving a torch.

RC But we've just heard that the world's most indecisive man was born today. He is forty-seven.

In the Chair Monologue

I was rummaging through a box of old documents the other day – I forget what I was looking for, no I don't – I'd had a little tiff with my wife and there was a little bit of high-spirited name-calling and I had stormed out of the room to fetch my birth certificate.

Actually I never did find it and when I asked my mother she confessed that when I was a baby I was so ugly – that's hard to believe isn't it?

Anyway I was so ugly that I never had a birth certificate, I had an invoice.

And she told me a little story. About once when she took me on a bus and the conductor came along for the fares and he

'Anyway, and this was what
I was coming to . . .'

looked at me and said 'Missus that's the ugliest child that I have ever seen,' he said, 'A joke is a joke but that kid is frightening!' So she gets rather upset and starts having a few tears.

She says, 'Stop the bus I want to get off.'

'With pleasure.'

And she gets off and sits on a seat outside a public house, still crying, boohoo, boohoo!

And she is sitting there a few minutes and she is making so much noise that a man comes out of the pub and he says to her, 'What's the matter?' And she is so upset that she can't speak, so he says, 'Stay there, I'll get you a drop of something to cheer you up a bit.'

And he goes back in the pub and he comes out and he says, 'Here you are Missus, I got a brandy for you and some nuts for the monkey.'

So as a child I led a very sheltered life, in fact every time I see a picture of a prisoner with a blanket over his head holding hands with a policeman it reminds me of going shopping with Mummy.

And I was fortunate that the first school I ever went to was a pretty soft school for pretty soft kids. Good heavens, at Saint Pansy's Primary you could have a reign of terror with a balloon on a stick. We were paying protection money to the Brownies. We were so sensitive that when a teacher said, 'Ding dong dell, pussy's down the well,' six of us fainted.

I remember that the worst thing that could happen to you at Saint Pansy's was to be selected for the school football team.

On a good day we used to lose by about a hundred to nil. Saint Pansy's was never really sports-oriented – when we played football our school strip was grey overcoats and black galoshes – and our trainer was the district nurse.

I often think we must have been an inspiring sight as we swept down the field in our four-two-one formation – and it was a pity we never had the ball with us.

And our goalkeeper never ever had a chance, he could only ever get one hand to the ball because his mother was holding the other one.

At half-time we used to have a bowl of
bread and milk and a good cry. We were so
nervous that if we were given a penalty
we'd let one of them take it for us.
Sometimes we used to stay out during half-
time and put a few through our own goal so
the other team would like us when they
came back on. I recall the last game I ever
played was against a local team, Saint
Margaret's.

My, they were big girls.

I think some of them had never seen a
boy before and they ran on to the field and
caught our winger and tried to take him to
pieces to see how he worked. Poor old
Larry Grayson's never been the same since.

Anyway that is really nothing at all to do
with what I was going to tell you about.

What I was going to say was that while me and the au pair were in the attic looking through these old papers, the au pair came across – rather an unfortunate phrase – she found an old invitation to the old boys' reunion at my senior school, the old Martin Boorman Comprehensive.

And that was one of the most exciting evenings I ever remember.

It all started very formally, we all sang the school song, 'Lily of Laguna', and the head-master led us into three cheers for penicillin.

Anyway, and this is what I was coming to. It was at the reception afterwards that I met this fantastic girl. Beautiful face, fantastic figure.

I said, 'Can I get you a drink?'
She said, 'No thank you, I don't drink.'
I said, 'Smoke?'
She said, 'No thank you, I don't.'
I said, 'Can I see you home?'
She said, 'Yes please.'

So we get to her house about ten minutes later and as we were standing in the doorway, I said to her, 'You are the most wonderful girl I have ever met, you don't drink or smoke, you're beautiful, intelligent, and have a wonderful sense of humour.'

She said, 'I'm also very passionate, would you like to come in?'

She opened the front door and there lying in the hall was a dead horse.

I said, 'What's that!?'

She said, 'I never said I was tidy, did I?'

Humphrey and Godfrey (1)

RB and RC in armchairs in their London club.

RC I say, Godfrey.

RB What is it, Humphrey?

RC How's your headache?

RB She's out playing bridge.

RC Come now, Godfrey, you shouldn't talk about the old gel like that, you know. Love makes the world go round.

RB So does a punch on the nose, old lad. No, I've had bad luck with both my wives. The first divorced me and the second one won't.

RC It was a case of love at first sight with me.

RB Then why didn't you marry her?

RC I saw her again on several occasions.

RB So you married someone else?

RC Yes, she's very slow.

RB Slow? What at?

RC Everything. It takes her a day to make instant coffee. Trouble is, I'm hen-pecked.

RB Oh! Mustn't be, old lad. Stand up to her. Show her who's boss.

RC I'm going to. I've made up my mind I'm going to pluck up courage and tell her something I've been wanting to tell her for ages.

RB What's that?

RC I must have a new apron!

'And news just in . . .'

Now Here Are the Announcements

RB   We've just been handed an urgent
warning about Trimmets Treacle
Puddings, which have caused several
people to be sent to hospital with
badly scalded feet. It seems people
have misunderstood the instructions
which read, 'Before opening tin, stand
in boiling water for twenty minutes.'

RC   The South Pilling Fire Brigade which
has been late for every fire in the last
seven years is seeking suggestions as to
what can be going wrong. If you've
any ideas please ring the Fire Brigade
at South Pilling 67421865992487164 –
extension 7787124 – and leave a
message on the answerphone.

We Were So Poor . . .

My wife came from a poor family as well – her father was a professional carol singer. When we got married even her wedding dress was army surplus.

In Politics

RB The Chancellor has announced new plans for shortening the dole queues. He's asking the men to stand closer together.

RC However, in a white paper today the Government revealed plans to help the small shopkeeper – a lower counter.

RB And the Prime Minister announced today a new plan to ensure we don't all suddenly become poor when we reach sixty – he's going to make sure we're all poor when we reach thirty.

In the Chair . . .

My great grandfather was killed at Custer's last stand – he didn't take part in the fighting, he was camping nearby and went over to complain about the noise.

Pismonuncers Unanimus

RB   Good evening. I am the president for the loyal society for the relief of sufferers from pismonunciation; for people who cannot say their worms correctly. Or who use the wrong worms entirely, so that other people cannot underhand a bird they are spraying. It's just that you open your mouse, and the worms come turbling out in wuk a say that you dick knock what you're thugging a bing, and it's very distressing. I'm always looing it, and it makes one feel umbumfterkookle; especially when going about one's diddly tasks – slopping in the sloopermarket, for inkstands. Only last wonk I approached the chuckout point, and showed the ghoul behind the crash desk the contents of my trilley, and she said, 'All right, granddad, shout 'em out.' Well, of course, that's fine for the ordinary man in the stoat, who has no dribble with his warts, but to someone like myself, it's worse than a kick in the jackstrop. Sometimes you get stuck on one letter, such as wubbleyou, and I said, 'I've got a tin of whoop, a woocumber, two packets of wees and a wallyflower.' She tried to make fun of me and said, 'That will be woo pounds and wifty wee pence.' So I said 'Wobblers' and walked out.

So you see how dickyfelt it is. But help is at hand. A new society has been formed by our mumblers to help each other in times of ex cream ices. It is bald 'Pismonuncers Unanimous' and anyone can ball them up on the smellyfone at any tight of the day or gnome, twenty-four flowers a spray, seven stays a creak, and they will come round and get you drunk. For foreigners, there will be interpreters who will all squeak many sandwiches, such as Swedish, Turkish, Burkish, Jewish, Gibberish and Rubbish. Membranes will be able to attend tight stool for heaving grasses, to learn how to grope with the many kerplinkities of daily loaf. Which brings me to the drain reason for squawking to you tonight.

The Society's first function, as a body, was a Grand Garden Freight, and we hope for many more bodily functions in the future. The Garden Plate was held in the grounds of Blenheim Paliasse, Woodstick, and guest of horror was the great American pip singer, Manny Barrowload. The fête was opened by the Bleeder of the Proposition, Mr Neil Pillock, who gave us a few well-frozen worms in praise of the Society's jerk,

COMEDY CLASSICS

and said that in the creaks and stunts that lie ahead, we must all do our nut-roast to ensure that it sucks weeds. Then everyone visited the various stalls and abruisements, the rudabouts, thingboats and dodgers, and of course the old favourites such as cocoshy nuts, stry your length, guessing the weight of the cook, and tinning the pail on the wonkey.

The occasional was great fun and, in short, I think it can safely be said that all the men present and thoroughly good women were had all the time.

So please join our Society. Write to me – Doctor Small Pith *(caption: 'DR PAUL SMITH')*, The Spanner, Poke Moses *(caption: 'THE MANOR, STOKE POGES')*, and I will send you some brieflets to browse through and a brass badge to wear in your loop-hole. And a very pud night to you all.

COMEDY CLASSICS

Business News

RC   A new electric car is to be withdrawn from the market. A spokesperson said, 'It was a failure. It could only travel three yards as the flex wasn't long enough.'

RB   But we've just had news of two important business mergers: Pye records have merged with Apple records to make Apple Pyes.

RC   And Krispie Bacon Limited has merged with Rolls-Royce to make Sausage Rolls and Royce Krispies.

In the Chair – We Were So Poor . . .

My mother only had a rusty gas ring on an upturned bucket to cook on. And every night she cooked a meal for twenty-eight of us. There were really only three of us in the family but she loved entertaining.

Humphrey and Godfrey (2)

RB and RC in armchairs in their London club.

RB (*looking at newspaper*) I say,
Humphrey.

RC What is it, Godfrey?

RB It says here, 'A firm bust in four weeks'.

RC That's nothing – my brother's firm
went bust in a fortnight.

RB No, no old boy, it's an advert – for
women.

RC Don't answer it, old chap, you've
already got one. Talking of women,
seen the new maid in the bar?

RB Yes. I've seen better legs on a piano. And with a piano, you get one extra. Bit of a gold-digger too.

RC Really?

RB Yes. I can read women like a book.

RC What system do you use?

RB Braille.

RC Trouble with life is, when you're young you can't afford women. By the time you have money to burn, the fire's gone out.

RB Like my brother. He still chases his secretaries round the desk but he can't remember why.

The Allotment

RB and RC sitting by some old boxes by a shed on an allotment. Sunny weather. They are slow-thinking, slow-talking country folk.

RB You know old Cyril Harris, with the one eye?

RC Yes. You don't see much of him lately.

RB   No, well he don't see much of us, either.

RC   No. Where did you see him then?

RB   Up the pictures. He went up to the girl in the box office there and he says, 'With one eye I should think you'd let me in for half price.' But she wasn't having it.

RC   Oh. Did he have to pay full price?

RB   He had to pay double.

RC   Double? Why was that then?

RB   She reckoned it would take him twice as long to see the picture.

RC   Oh.

(They think this over.)

This Just In – Incidents & Accidents

RB Temperance Toyshops are to withdraw a thousand-piece nude jigsaw of Tom Jones unless seventy-three pieces are withdrawn.

RC In the English Channel a ship carrying red paint collided with a ship carrying purple paint. It is believed that both crews have been marooned.

RB And there was an accident involving Britain's worst goalkeeper, Bill Berkely, who has already let through 157 goals this season. Shouting out 'I am a complete failure,' Berkeley threw himself in front of a bus . . . luckily the bus passed under him and he wasn't hurt.

RC There was a nasty accident at a Hollywood bowling alley today when Telly Savalas bent down to do up a shoelace. A passer-by stuck two fingers up his nostrils.

News from the Awards

RB   Today's anniversaries:
Jimmy Tarbuck had a
telegram from the Queen
today. His jokes were
exactly one hundred
years old.

RC   And shy spinster Hester
Pettigrew was awarded
the George Cross for saving
the life of a drowning man.
She gave him the kiss of life
with her bicycle pump.

RB But Sir Wilbury Chintz, the famous upholstery expert who yesterday fell into a fabric loom, is said to be almost completely recovered.

RC Now a sketch in which Mr Ronnie Barker plays the part of a bridegroom who finds there is no bed in the honeymoon suite and has to stand up for his conjugal rights.

In the Chair – My Wife

I was talking to my wife this morning – I was
– fame hasn't changed me a bit – still
unspoiled – lovable – God, the autographs
I've given that woman. Anyway I was talking
to her this morning – and she was talking to
me – personally – a sort of private audience
– where will it all end?

I said to her, 'Mrs Corbett—'

D'you ever feel you're drifting apart?

Society Gossip

RC   A new report from the Society for Perfect Printing states that 'British printing is food and getting butter every day. This is due to the fact that all the balley poofs get careful studs.'

RB   There's less good news from the National Conference of Henpecked Husbands at the South Norwood Astrodome. The conference failed to turn up. It had to go and mow the lawn.

RC   Better news from the West Ham Short-Sighted Society. They held a picnic on Clapham Common . . . And the East Ham Short-Sighted Society held a picnic on the West Ham Short-Sighted Society.

The Allotment

*RB and RC sitting by some old boxes by a
shed on an allotment. Sunny weather. They
are slow-thinking, slow-talking country folk.*

RC   Didn't old Charlie go to the doctor's
       with his ears?

RB   That's right, yes.

RC   Deaf, wasn't he?

RB   Eh?

RC   Deaf.

COMEDY CLASSICS

RB He was, yes.

RC Did the doctor improve his hearing?

RB Must have done. He's just heard from his brother in America.

RC Oh.

(They think this over.)

An Appeal for Women

RB   Good evening. My name is Arnold Splint, and I am here tonight. *(Caption – 'An appeal for Women'.)* This is an appeal for women only. No, please don't switch off – because it's you men I want to talk to, especially tonight. I am appealing to you, for women. I need them desperately. I can't get enough – and the reason I'm appealing to you men is that I don't appeal to women. But I still need them.

So this is how you can help. If you have an old woman you no longer need – send her to me. Simply tie her arms and legs together, wrap her in brown paper, and post her to me, care of the BBC, with your own name printed clearly on the bottom. Because that's the bit I shall undo first. Of course, I cannot guarantee to make use of all women sent to me. It depends on the condition, so make sure you enclose a self-addressed pair of knickers. Send as many women as you like, no matter how small. I assure you, all those accepted will be made good use of by me and my team of helpers – who, incidentally, carry on this work, many without any form of support.

I do hope you can find time to send me something: we did originally start collecting with a van, from door to door, but this scheme was abandoned owing to the wear and tear on the knockers.

I think we should remember that Christmas is on its way. And when it comes, and you are sitting at home by your own fireside, warming yourself beside a roaring great woman, think of all those poor unfortunate people who are having to go without this Christmas. Why not send them an old flame or two, to warm the cockles of their hearthrug? I'm quite sure that many of you have women lying about in drawers, that you haven't touched for years. Please, post them off today.

Help us set up our Women On Wheels service for old men who can't move about. I know it's not easy. It requires self-denial, patience and an enormous amount of string; but I'm sure you'll feel better for it. I know I shall.

Goodnight.

But There's Bad News from . . .

RC Manchester, where a teacher with special responsibility for sex education at a comprehensive school today eloped with one of his visual aids.

RB And by the way, later in the programme, Monsieur Pierre Bouffon, France's most amorous football manager, will tell us of his club's progress in the European Cup, and why he's always glad to get the first leg over.

Humphrey and Godfrey (3)

RB and RC in armchairs, in their London club.

RB I say, Humphrey.

RC What is it, Godfrey?

RB You know, no matter how hot the day is, at night it gets dark.

RC Yes. It's the same in America.

RB Just come back, haven't you?

RC Mm.

RB Did you go for pleasure, or did the wife go with you?

RC Went alone. Very grand hotel.

RB Really?

RC Yes. So grand that even the guests have to use the service entrance.

RB   That is grand.

RC   Funny people, the Americans, though. On the plane going over, a woman collapsed. Doctor, sitting on one side of her, refused to help. Said he was on holiday.

RB   Amazing.

RC   Chap sitting other side of her said, 'That's disgraceful.' Doctor said, 'Would you carry on your profession if you were on holiday?' 'I certainly would,' said the other chap. 'All right, what is your profession?' he said. 'I'm a fishmonger,' said the other chap, and he picked the woman up, loosened her clothing and sold her two pounds of haddock.

In the Chair – We Were So Poor . . .

For my birthday my parents had given me an old bra and told me it was a double-barrelled catapult.

Today in the Courts

RC A journalist who slandered the Chancellor of the Exchequer very badly was given a chance to do better in the High Court today.

RB A man who ate scampi contaminated with mercury successfully sued the Alpha Bottled Scampi Co. for injuries. He said every time the temperature went up he hit his head on the ceiling.

RC Finally, a man complained of the noise made by the amorous couple in the flat above him. Each evening they'd sing 'The Red Flag', eat their supper, have fun on the sofa and take a very naughty bath together—

RB —So every night it was hammer and sickle, cheese and pickle, slap and tickle and bubble and squeak.

Mark My Words

A pub. RB at bar, drinking a pint – flat cap.
RC enters – flat cap. They speak throughout
without any sign of emotion at all.

RC Evening, Harry.

RB Hullo, Bert.

RC I just been up the doctor's. I've been
having a bit of trouble with my, er—

RB Chest?

RC No, with my—

RB Back?

RC No—

RB   Side?

RC   No—

RB   Backside?

RC   No, my wife.

RB   Oh.

RC   My wife. She seems to have got it into
her head that I'm a, I'm a—

RB   What, annoyed
with her?

RC   No, a—

RB   A Martian?

RC No—

RB A poof?

RC No, a bit under the weather. But he's examined me all over. Nothing wrong at all. He told me to drop my—

RB Really?

RC And he looked at my—

RB Go on.

RC And he said there was nothing to worry about at all. No, on the contrary, he said I was, er— I was er—

RB First class?

RC   No—

RB   Fascinating?

RC   No—

RB   Friendly?

RC   No, fit.

RB   Oh, fit.

RC   Perfectly fit for a—

RB   Change.

RC   No, for a man of—

RB   Ninety?

RC For a man of my age. It's nice to know, isn't it? 'Cos I only went up there on the—

RB Bus?

RC No, on the off chance.

RB Oh, off chance, yes.

RC I tell you who was up there. That young Julie.

RB Julie?

RC Yeah, you know. Her mother's got them big, er—

RB Teeth?

RC No, them big—

RB Bay windows?

RC No, them big Alsatians. You know, them ones she keeps taking up the common and they keep biting people in the er—

RB Leg?

RC No, in the er—

RB Bushes?

RC No, in the evenings. Well, her kid, Julie. She was up there.

RB Oh, what was she up there for?

RC Well, she was telling me, she went out one night with some young lad, and they fell in the duck pond, and now she's er—

RB Pregnant?

RC No, er—

RB Stagnant?

RC No, now she's er—

RB Fragrant?

RC No, she's off work with a cut foot. Doctor said she was lucky, with that duck pond, it could've been a lot worse. It could have been a septic er—

RB Septic tank?

RC Toenail. Septic toenail.

'We interrupt this bulletin . . .'

In the Chair – The Producer's Party (1)

So we are all round the producer's house, about ten of us, just his friends and a few extras from an agency to fill the place up a bit.

Anyway we're having a great time – I'm standing there, glass of wine, cigar and the *Daily Mirror*.

A couple of them are dancing to a recording of a speech by Sir Winston Churchill. And the producer's wife is circulating among the guests trying to sell souvenir pictures of her wedding night.

So right, the party is just going along nicely because his parties can get a bit dreary – I remember the last one, a light bulb blew out and we were still laughing about it two hours later.

The Allotment

RB and RC sitting by some old boxes by a shed on an allotment. Sunny weather. They are slow-thinking, slow-talking country folk.

RC   I see that Mrs Parkinson got her divorce. Her that's got that husband on the stage.

RB   Oh, yes?

RC   They gave her the divorce 'cos he snored.

RB   You can't get a divorce for snoring, can you?

RC   Ah well, you see her husband was a
ventriloquist and he snored on her
side of the bed.

RB   Oh.

(They think this over.)

But First the News

RB We've gleaned the following items of news by listening to two short-wave radio stations at once. We haven't had time to edit so here we go

RC The President of Caramba arrived today. He was—

RB —wearing a fawn-coloured raincoat and had a scar over his left ear. A lady explorer just back from Ethiopia tells how a few years ago she lost all her clothes in a tropical rainstorm. She then met an important man and realised to her embarrassment that he was in fact Haile—

RC —delighted. The President of the Newport Camden Family Planning Association is to have yet another child.

COMEDY CLASSICS

RB —anyone who saw the accident is asked to phone Scotland Yard, Whitehall one—

RC —Arsenal three. In the Miss World competition today Miss Sweden was placed first. A close second was—

RB —Mr Michael Foot. The Commons then debated the price of syrup of figs but—

RC —only three ran. In the Gloria van Crumpett divorce case the correspondent was named as—

RB —the Argyll and Sutherland Highlanders with the help of the Highland Light Infantry.

RC But here's a special announcement. The government is to levy VAT on words. This means that a lot of words will have to be shorter. Now here's tomorrow's news:

The Quee and the Duk of Ed flew by Conc last nig to visit Mr Cart. Meanwhile at Cow yac race in his bra new yac. Lat footba res: Tott Hot two, Arse nil.

RB Here is a newsflash just in: Milk bottles were thrown at a meeting of the Milk Marketing Board this afternoon and a meeting of the Egg Marketing Board was also broken up when eggs were thrown. A mass meeting of the Manure Marketing Board has been cancelled.

We Interrupt This Bulletin

RB *For a police message. Will the man who lost eight bottles of whisky at Euston Station this morning please go to the Lost Property office by Platform Nine where the man who found them has just been handed in.*

In the Chair – The Producer's Party (2)

Anyway we'd just about exhausted the entertainment possibilities – we'd all had a ride in the lift. And the producer had just done his rather tasteless send-up of the head of BBC Light Entertainment. And my wife, who is going through a sticky patch at the moment, was putting milk bottles down the waste disposal. And someone said, 'What shall we do now?'

Well I was feeling a bit full of myself – I found out later that someone had been putting metal polish in my glass of Vin du Sennapod. By the time I'd found out who was doing it, the tin was empty. Anyway, I said tipsily, 'I know what we can do, why don't we all hold hands and try to get in touch with the living?'

The World of Medicine

RB The Family Planning Association
announces that in Britain 90% of all
parents are, or have been, on the Pill.

RC And 85% of them are women. Of these
85%, 20% are now on it and 13% are
now off it, 12% are on it on and off
and 9% are off it off and on, 8% are
often on it, 7% are often off it, 6% are
off it and wish they were on it and 4%
are on it and off it so seldom it doesn't
matter. 3% are don't knows, 2% are
don't cares, 1% are no! don't!s and
Mrs Ivy Whizzer was disqualified for
ruining her entrance form.

The Allotment

RB and RC sitting by some old boxes by a shed on an allotment. Sunny weather. They are slow-thinking, slow-talking country folk.

RC   Do you reckon we live longer now than we used to?

RB   Oh yes, undoubtedly. I've never lived so long in my life. That's 'cos they've gone back to breast-feeding, you know.

RC   Oh?

RB   Yes. Mother's milk is much better than cow's milk.

RC   How d'you reckon that then?

RB   Well, it's always fresh and the cat can't get at it.

RC   Yes.

RB   And it comes in handy little containers.

RC   Yes.

RB   And you don't have to leave them out for the milkman.

RC *(after a pause)* The woman next door does.

RB Oh.

(They think this over.)

An Odd Couple

Two gents in a slightly shabby living room. RC in his vest and trousers, ironing a shirt. RB enters in his vest, drying his hair – he has just washed it.

RB   'Ere, Tony.

RC   What?

RB   You remember old Mr Whatsisname who used to come to the pub?

RC   Who?

RB   Used to come in with that big woman, you know.

News from the Art World

RC   *The engagement was today announced between the famous post impressionist Madeleine Renoir and Mr Percy Edwards, the famous animal impersonator. They met when he was giving his impression of a dog and she was giving her impression of a post.*

RB   *The Boston Bean Ensemble is to amalgamate with the Boston Radish Ensemble to form the Boston Wind Ensemble.*

RC   I don't know who you mean.

RB   Big woman, wore a fur coat. Lives near Dennis's mother.

RC   Dennis who?

RB   Dennis. Masses of dark hair; big with it; sallow boy. Worked for that printing firm in Surbiton.

RC   What printing firm?

RB   The firm that was supposed to do all Winston Churchill's visiting cards during the war.

RC Who?

RB Winston Churchill. The war leader!
Ooh, my Gawd! The chap who saved
us from the clutches of Adolf.

RC Adolf who?

RB Hitler. Adolf Hitler. Don't tell me you
don't know who Adolf Hitler was.

RC 'Course I know who Adolf Hitler was.
I'm not a moron, Harold.

RB Well, then.

RC Well, what?

RB Well, he's dead.

RC Who, Hitler?

RB No! (Hitler!) You silly queen! I was saying Churchill saved us from Hitler.

RC What about it?

RB I was just saying Churchill used to get all his visiting cards done by this firm where Dennis worked.

RC Dennis who?

RB I'm trying to tell you. The fellah whose mother lives near this big woman with a fur coat.

RC   What big woman?

RB   The WOMAN who used to COME IN
THE PUB with old Mr Whatsisname.

RC   Turner.

RB   TURNER! MR TURNER! HIM, YES!

RC   What about him?

RB   HE'S DEAD!

RC   They never proved it. He might be
living under another name in South
America.

The Allotment

RB and RC sitting by some old boxes by a shed on an allotment. Sunny weather. They are slow-thinking, slow-talking country folk.

RB You know that woman lives over the back of Tomkin's?

RC Oh, ah. She's got a bright pink Mini.

RB How do you know?

RC I seen her in it.

RB Oh.

RC Why, what about her?

RB Eh?

RC What about her?

RB Oh. Well, old Jack says she was always after her husband to buy her a Jaguar.

RC Well?

RB Well, he did, and it ate her.

RC Oh.

(They ruminate.)

That's What I Said

RC and girl sitting up at L-shaped bar. RB enters. Large-bosomed barmaid approaches him. She wears a very low-cut sweater.

RB *(to barmaid)* Good evening. Tickle your botty with a feather tonight.

BARMAID I beg your pardon?

RB Particularly grotty weather tonight.

BARMAID Oh. Yes, isn't it.

RB That sweater looks a little risky.

BARMAID Pardon?

RB I said, I'd better have a little whisky.

BARMAID Oh. I thought you said
            something about my sweater.

RB No, no – that's very nice.

BARMAID Thank you.

RB Mustn't get the hiccups or they'll fall
        out.

BARMAID What did you say?

RB I said, I've just heard the cricket score, they're all out.

RB moves over to RC and girl, who had her arm round RC's neck.

RB Who's this silly ass with the ugly daughter?

RC I beg your pardon?

RB I said, I wonder if you'd pass the jug of water.

RC Oh.

He does so.

RB Thanks awfully, you dozy fish-face.

RC Pardon?

RB I said, thanks – awfully cosy, this place.

RC You know, if you don't mind my saying so, you seem to sound as if you're saying things other than what you say you are saying, if you understand me.

RB *(indicating his large moustache)* Oh dear – I'm afraid it's this moustache, it sort of muffles the sound. My wife likes it so, otherwise I'd shave it off, and drown it in the sink.

GIRL   Otherwise you'd what?

RB   Shave it off – I'm sounding indistinct.

GIRL   Oh, quite.

RB   You're a nice girl – do you drop 'em,
for a friend?

GIRL   What?!

RB I said, have you dropped in on your friend?

GIRL Oh, no, he's my boss. He's an accountant.

RB Oh, I see. My name's Gollinson, by the way. I sell long hooters to alligators.

RC You what?

RB I sell computers and calculators. So this is your secretary, eh?

RC Yes – we're working late at the office.

RB Ah! Going back for a tease and a cuddle.

RC Yes, we're going back because the VAT's in a muddle. Miss Jones is new – I had to sack my last girl.

RB Why, did she ignore your advances?

RC That's it, yes. She was a big bore at dances.

RB I bet this one's a right little goer.

RC Yes, she does write a little slower, but I don't mind.

RB I know the type – she's one of the 'mad with desire' brigade.

RC How funny you should know that!

RB What?

RC Her dad's in the fire brigade. Well, we must go. I want to look up your skirt and down your dress.

GIRL Eh?

RC I want to look up Lord Burton's town address.

GIRL I think it's somewhere in my drawers.

RB That sounds like an invitation. If I were you, I'd lurch through those doors and get her back to the office.

RC   I will. I'll search through her drawers and get her a bag of toffees.

The girl exits with RC.

BARMAID Funny sort of chap.

RB   Yes. But let's talk about you. You'll never drown, with those water wings.

BARMAID I beg your pardon?

RB   You should wear brown with those sort of things.

BARMAID It's not really your moustache –
you're actually saying those
things on purpose, aren't you?

RB Only trying to drum up a little trade,
that's all.

BARMAID What sort of trade?

RB I sell deaf-aids.

In the Chair – Back to the Joke

Anyway, back to the joke which I'd like to dedicate to my grandfather whom I'm afraid we've just lost. My wife left him outside Tesco's and when she came out he was gone.

We gave the police a full description of him and they decided he wasn't worth looking for.

The Allotment

RB and RC sitting by some old boxes by a shed on an allotment. Sunny weather. They are slow-thinking, slow-talking country folk.

RB   You still getting that dizziness when you wake up of a morning?

RC   Yes, I am.

RB   How long do it last?

RC   About half an hour. Then I'm all right after that.

RB You been to the doctor about it?

RC Yes.

RB What did he say?

RC He told me to sleep half an hour longer.

RB Oh.

(They think this over.)

We Interrupt This Bulletin

RC British customs officials have arrested a famous Russian woman spy after the discovery of two miniature radios hidden in the cups of her bra. Said an official, 'We became suspicious when from the top of her dress we heard Kenneth McKellar singing "The Hills Are Alive with the Sound of Music".'

Fat-Heads Revisited

Two yokels meet by the barn. RB sitting, RC enters.

RC Morning.

RB Arternoon.

RC Is somebody sitting here?

RB Yes.

RC Who?

RB Me.

RC Well, I know that. I'm not daft.

RB I am. *(Noticing RC limping)* What's making you limp?

RC I'm not limp.

RB No, your feet. Lost a shoe?

RC *(holding up both feet)* No. Just found one.

RB Oh. Lucky it fits.

RC Bound to fit one of my feet. One of my feet's bigger than the other. Everybody has one foot bigger than the other.

RB I haven't. I'm just the opposite.

RC Eh?

RB One of my feet is smaller than the other. Ain't you got no shoes?

RC I got me best shoes. For Sundays, like. I bought a new tie an' all. But I had to take it back.

RB Why?

RC It were too tight.

RC notices a front door leaning against the wall behind RB.

RC What's that door?

RB I take that around with me.

RC What for?

RB Well, the other day I lost the key, so in case anybody finds it and breaks into my house, I carry the door around.

RC That's clever. But what happens if you lose the door?

RB That's all right, I've left a window open.

RC Here, did you hear about old Reuben?

RB What?

RC Up in court yesterday.

RB   Never.

RC   He stole a calendar.

RB   What did he get?

RC   Twelve months. His trouble is, he drinks too much.

RB   He told me he only drinks to calm himself.

RC   Oh well, that explains it. Last Saturday night he was so calm he couldn't move.

RB   Here. It's my birthday tomorrow. November the twelfth.

RC   What year?

RB Oh, every year. I had two presents. A wristwatch with an alarm, and a bottle of aftershave. So if you hear anything and smell anything, it's me.

RC Oh, ar. Well, at least you won't be late for work. I'm always late for work.

RB Why's that?

RC I sleep very slowly.

RB I snore, I do. I snore so loud I wake meself up. But I've cured it now.

RC How?

RB I sleep in the next room.

RC Here, talking of snoring, it's my wife's birthday next week. She's asked for a coat made of animal skin.

RB What you going to give her?

RC A donkey jacket.

RB That's nice. Here, this is another present I got.

Shows umbrella, opens it. It has a four-inch circular hole in one section of it.

RC What's that hole for?

RB So you can see when it's stopped raining.

Society Gossip . . .

RC   *The Annual General Meeting of the Claustrophobia Society at the Albert Hall was a fiasco. Only one member turned up and he kept shouting, 'Let me out!'*

RC Here, seeing that hole reminds me. I looked through an hole in the fence up at that new nudist camp.

RB Ooh ar, I've heard about that. Do they have men and women in there?

RC I couldn't tell. They hadn't got any clothes on.

RB Oh, I see.

RC Well, I must sit here. I'm going up to the doctor's. I don't like the look of my wife.

RB I'll come with you. I hate the sight of mine.

They exit.

The Allotment

RB and RC sitting by some old boxes by a shed on an allotment. Sunny weather. They are slow-thinking, slow-talking country folk.

RB   Here, you know we live in the same sort of house?

RC   Yes.

RB   Same road, same shape, same size rooms?

RC   Yes.

RB You know when you wallpapered your front room and you told me you bought eight rolls of wallpaper?

RC That's right, yes.

RB Well, I just papered our front room.

RC Oh, yes?

RB I bought eight rolls of wallpaper and when I finished, I had two rolls over.

RC That's funny. So did I.

RB Oh.

(He thinks about this.)

And News from the Zoos

RC   We've just heard sensational news from Whipsnade. The male panda, who's developed a passion for music, has mated with the head keeper's harmonium. Experts say this may create a pandamonium.

The Sex Equality Monologue

RB discovered as spokesman – dressed half as a man and half as a woman. Half a long blonde wig, half a black moustache, half a frilly dress, half a suit jacket, half a bosom.

COMEDY CLASSICS

RB   Good evening. I'm from the Ministry of Sex Equality, and I'm here tonight to explain the situation man to man – or as we have to say now – person to person.

My name is Mr Stroke Mrs Barker. But I don't advise any of you to try it. Stroking Mrs Barker, that is. Now due to this new law, no one is allowed to be called male or female, man or woman. This has already caused a great deal of argument in Parliament, so they are all going for a Parliamentary conference at Personchester. They will all stay at a nudist colony and air their differences. Members only, of course.

But where do you come in? Is it easy to become unsexed? Well, it can be done. And I represent the proof. At least, half of me does, the other half's quite normal. The first thing we have to realise is that for too long, women have been beneath men – not only in the home, but at the office. And there are many ways in which we can change that. Vertical desktops for a start. The main area of change, of course, will be in the language. The 'man in the street' will become the 'person in the street'. Whoever you are, whether man or woman, you will be the person in the street. Incidentally, when I was in the street the other day, I nearly fell down a personhole, so be careful.

Certain professions will have their names changed. From the Chairperson of a large company, right down to the humble Dustperson. (Not to be confused, of course, with the famous film star, Dustin Hoffperson.) Speaking of films, there will be special feature films made, showing the equality of the sexes. Already in production, a new musical called *Seven Persons For*

Seven Other Persons starring Paul Newperson and Robert Help-person, with music by Persontovani and His Orchestra.

Now, dress. Of course, you won't be expected to dress like this. This sort of costume is much too expensive. Half a knicker certainly doesn't cover it. No, each person can of course choose what to wear, provided it includes the customary shirt, bra, underpants and a handbag. Shoes can be black or brown, according to individual taste. I myself find that black shoes taste better than brown shoes.

Jobs, too, will be entirely sexless, with one or two obvious exceptions. What are they, you may ask? You may ask, but I'm not telling you on this programme. But here is a clue. They have jam on them, and appear at teatime. A job must be open to either a whatsit or a whoosit – that is, of either sex. For instance, certain advertisements will not be allowed. This one here says *(holds up newspaper cutting)* 'Bar staff required for West Country pub, male or female. Must have big boobs.' Now that won't be passed by the Ministry at all. What they should have said was 'Bar staff required, male or female. Must be attractive in the Bristol area.' That would have got past.

A recent idea by the Ministry, to avoid confusion, is to call a man a doings, and a woman a thingy. This offends no one, and makes conversation clearer. Thus we instantly recognise the book called *Little Thingies* or the play by George Bernard Shaw called *Doings and Superdoings*. There are times, however, when it sounds better to stick to the word 'person'. 'The person in the street' is still better than 'The doings in the street'. That is something to look out for and steer clear of.

Finally, don't let this new law alter your life. After all, what's in a name? As the great John Greenpimple once remarked – a rose by any other name doth smell as sweet. Or a Henry.

Goodnight.

In The Chair Monologue – We Were So Poor . . .

My father was twenty-seven years down the mine and his dinner was still in the oven.

Crime News

RB   Reports are coming in of a big jewel raid said to have been committed by Sooty. Harry Corbett is believed to have had a hand in it.

RC   A man was charged today with eccentric behaviour in certain London streets. He went to Pudding Lane and made a pudding of himself, he went to Gooseberry Lane and made a fool of himself, then he went to Exhibition Road and got himself arrested.

RB Mr Lemuel Shift, described as the world's sneakiest little man, denied today that he'd been to Scotland Yard to take a lie detector test. If there was one missing, he said, it was nothing to do with him.

RC A thief broke into a men's outfitter's in London. He stole only a truss and a straw boater. Police are looking for a very careful tap dancer.

RB There was a fracas in London in the small hours of this morning, involving a Seamus O'Higgins. After a lengthy argument O'Higgins was arrested by PC Wallace Gudgeon who claimed his nose was broken in three places – Marble Arch, Piccadilly Circus and Tower Bridge.

RC   And more than one hundred policemen, searching for stolen jewellery, dragged Staines Reservoir for three hours. They dragged it as far as the River Thames where it fell in.

The Allotment

RB and RC sitting by some old boxes by a shed on an allotment. Sunny weather. They are slow-thinking, slow-talking country folk.

RC Here.

RB What?

RC You know you told me the doctor said you could only have two pints a day?

RB That's right, yes.

RC   Well, your missus tells me you have half a dozen.

RB   Yes, that's right.

RC   How come?

RB   I went to two other doctors, and they each allow me two pints as well.

RC   Oh.

(They ruminate.)

You Can Say That Again

A pub. RB at bar. RC enters.

RB   Hello, Bert – what are you going to have?

RC   Oh, hello, Charlie. I'll have a pint of, er—

RB   Light?

RC   No, a pint of—

RB   Brown?

RC   No, a pint of—

RB   Mild?

RC   No—

RB Bitter?

RC Pint of bitter.

RB Pint of bitter. Pint of bitter, Alan. Haven't seen you round the factory lately – been off sick?

RC No, I packed it in. They told me I had to change me, er, change me, er—

RB Hours?

COMEDY CLASSICS

RC No, change me—

RB Habits?

RC No, change me—

RB Socks more often?

RC No, duties.

RB Oh, duties.

RC Change my duties, that's it. Well, I wasn't having that, 'cos I had a good job. Cushy little number. *(Barman delivers pint.)* Ta. Cheers.

Society Diary

RB At the big Fancy Dress Ball last night given by the Football Pools Federation, a young lady arrived entirely naked except for a cross marked on each bosom. She was allowed in when she explained that she was a chest of draws.

RB Cheers, Bert. What exactly was your job then, there?

RC Same job as I'd done for twenty years. I always worked with, er—

RB Pride?

RC No, I worked with, er—

RB Within reason?

RC No, with, er—

RB With your overcoat on?

RC No, with Harry Hawkins.

RB Oh, Harry Hawkins, yes.

RC We always worked together. He used to give me his, er—

RB Wholehearted support?

RC No, his, er—

RB Athletic support?

RC No, his ginger nuts.

RB Oh, nice.

RC And I used to dip them in, er—

RB His tea for him?

RC No, in the chocolate.

RB Oh, the chocolate, I see. That's the job, is it?

RC Me and him made all the chocolate ginger nuts. Then suddenly they decide a woman can do my job, and they put me on to, er—

RB Short time?

RC No, on to—

RB Shortcake?

RC No, sherbert fountains. Messy job, that, dreadful. Everything gets covered in it. You go home, strip off, and find you've got a coating of sherbert all over, er—

RB All over the weekend.

RC Precisely. And the wife doesn't like it.

RB Oh, that makes it worse. So you can't even—

RC Meanwhile, the woman refused to work with Harry Hawkins. She didn't like the way he handled his, er—

RB His ginger nuts?

RC His machinery, and she thought he
was, er—

RB Nuts?

RC No, she thought he was, er—

RB Ginger?

RC No, incompetent.

RB Oh, incompetent, yes. So you went
back with Harry, did you?

RC No, I decided I'd had enough. I went home to the wife and I found she was up, er—

RB Up to her knees in sherbert?

RC No, up, er—

RB Up to her old tricks with the milkman?

RC No, up her mother's. So I thought, why not go up the Job Centre?

RB So you're still out of work, are you?

RC No, they only had one post available, so I took it.

Later on this evening we'll be talking to . . .

RB . . . Mr Herbert Gudge who has tattooed the whole of his body with old masters. He has a Botticelli on his chest, a Constable under each arm, a Watteau down the back, a Whistler up the front – and the inscrutable smile of the Mona Lisa becomes a broad grin whenever he sits down . . .

RB Go on—

RC Yes, I've now got a job with the sweet, er—

RB With the sweet factory again?

RC No, a city job – a job with the sweet, er—

RB With the sweet smell of success?

RC Not exactly. I'm in charge of the Gents at Waterloo Station! Cheers!

The Allotment

RB and RC sitting by some old boxes by a shed on an allotment. Sunny weather. They are slow-thinking, slow-talking country folk.

RB Here, I've just read an extraordinary thing.

RC What's that?

RB Every time I breathe, a man dies.

RC Oh dear. You want to try chewing cloves.

RB Oh.

(They ruminate.)

And Then We'll Talk to the Man Who Crossed . . .

RC A skunk with a koala and got a poo bear.

RB Then he crossed a truss with a Polo mint and got a Nutcracker Suite

RC —And a Morse code transmitter with a senna pod and got dot dot dot and a very quick dash.

RB He even crossed a food mixer with a nymphomaniac with a lisp – and got a girl who'll whisk anything.

RC And a feather with a lady contortionist and got a girl who can tickle her own fancy.

RB And he actually crossed a table-tennis ball with an extremely tall chamber-pot and got a ping pong piddle-high poc.

RC Then we talk to a man who crossed a Gordon Highlander with a mousetrap and got a squeaky jockstrap.

RB And to a scientist from Kuwait who's bred an ostrich with a corkscrew head. You give it a fright and it drills for oil.

Well That's All For This Week.
Next Week . . .

RB By way of light relief we'll be taking a look at fur-covered toilet seats and asking: do they tickle your fancy?

RC We'll show you the new Mafia scarecrow. It's so terrifying, not only do the birds not take any seeds, they bring back the seeds they took last year.

RB Well, that's the end of another series, now we go our separate ways. Ronnie Corbett will be appearing in *The Two Gentlemen of Verona* at the public baths in Looe and I'll be appearing in *The Two Public Looes of Verona* in the Gentlemen's at Bath.

RC And that's all we've got room for in this book, isn't it, Ronnie?

RB Yes it is and that means it's . . .

'Goodnight from me . . .'

'And it's goodnight from him . . .'

'GOODNIGHT!'